Old Well Salted Wounds

A Slim Volume of Poetry

BY
RICHARD K. TOBIN

First Edition

Biographical Publishing Company
Prospect, Connecticut

OLD WELL SALTED WOUNDS
A SLIM VOLUME OF POETRY
First Edition

Published by:

Biographical Publishing Company
95 Sycamore Drive
Prospect, CT 06712-1493

Phone: 203-758-3661   Fax: 253-793-2618
e-mail: biopub@aol.com

All rights reserved. No part of this book may be reproduced or transmitted in any form or by any means, electronic or mechanical, including photocopying, recording, or by any information storage or retrieval system without the written permission of the author, except for the inclusion of brief quotations in a review.

Copyright © 2012 Richard K. Tobin
First Printing 2012
PRINTED IN THE UNITED STATES OF AMERICA

Publisher's Cataloging-in-Publication Data

Tobin, Richard K.
Old Well Salted Wounds: A Slim Volume of Poetry/ by Richard K. Tobin.
1st ed.
p. cm.
ISBN 1929882785 (alk. Paper)
13-Digit ISBN 9781929882786
1. Title. 2. Poetry, inspirational
Dewey Decimal Classification: 811 Canadian Poetry
BISAC Subjects:
    POE005000   POETRY / Single Author / General
    POE000000   POETRY / General
    POE003000   POETRY / Inspirational
Library of Congress Control Number: 2012918798

Forward
By the Poet, Richard K. Tobin

In this book of poetry, I try to mention quite regularly how difficult it is just to survive the many pains and hardships and blows of all kind. Things like a busted marriage, a broken romance, betrayal, being out of work, I could go on.

Despite the fact that we are basically a multicultural society, people of one kind refuse to accept the differences in another segment of society. I also mention corruption and failure of some of our once treasured institutions.

These poems gathered here, if nothing else, should keep you entertained and amused while you read along. Quite regularly, you will find that I think much like you do; it's just that I put it into words for the both of us.

Thank you, and I shall close off now, but before I do, remember no matter what, we can all still have hope.

A Poet's Search For That Ever So Elusive Emotion

This poem is based on the cover art of a well-known mystery magazine that was published in the summer of 2011. I was a subscriber at the time. It featured two young lovers standing on the deck of a yacht in more southerly climes. The rest is all pure imagination.

The iridescent sun
glowed radiantly in the sea blue sky
and shimmered over your golden hair.
The triangular canvas sail fluttered
under the gentle, steady, tutelage
of the soft, warm, island breezes.
The water lapped rhythmically
against the port side of the creamy white yacht
and you the ethereal jasmine stood by
my side in your black bikini
and a top adorable in blue stripes.
A sailor's dream, you were, ashore
in his favorite port, a love call
from his island girl
of the peach white skin.
May it never end for all eternity
but it will, oh yes, it will!
The ocean floor holds the secrets of bygone lovers
but now the whitened sand beach beckons
and perfumed flowers tickle the air caressingly.
The island calls to come back, come home,
so let us sup and go to
bed early, in case
tomorrow never comes, and we sail
alone through the darkened sky of dying love,
ebbing and flowing like
they who had cleaved on together
But heart sore drifted away.

Mary

This poem was inspired by a song about a man wistfully reflecting on a love gone wrong. The word 'bairn' and the expression 'ciad mille failte' are Gaelic in origin, being handed down from generation to generation from the earliest Scottish settlers until today, here on Cape Breton Island, along the east coast of Canada.

How long has it been Mary
Since you and I were young.
Your four bairns grown up and gone.
To you Mary I repeat
These words, ciad mille failte,
You are always welcome here.

How I remember we both
Sitting by the warming hearth
Hearts aglow in Grandfather Neil's cabin on the firth.
Drinking mulled wine and talking
About your college, so smart you were.
Your children clinging on the vine,
How I wish your children had been mine.
I dream of you and wish you well,
And pray and hope that perhaps some day
We, permission granted, can do it again a better way.

Reality Only Confuses Me

This poem was inspired in its entirety by a short story written by the master, Stephen King. I can't recall the name of that particular story, but it was a part of a collection of his superb short stories. I wish I could say the same for my poem.

Dinosaurs can fly
through the sky to
other galaxies
but so can the shy fly
to Washington Square
or tell a big white lie
or the Vietnam War's
memorial to the house of the dead.
corn on the cob can fly
on cool moonlit days,
the sun a pink horse with
a blue and silver saddle,
flying I guess above the earth
or out of my mind or
leaving straight society behind.
out of kilter
in a world gone helter skelter
be your own man (woman)
the genes are there.
do what you want to do,
and bring a harmonica with you.
blow and breathe
I say goodnight and goodbye,
my airborne liege and I.

Long and Bittersweet

Basically what we have here, you, the reader and I, is an abstract poem concerning a stormy romance gone sour. However, in abstract poetry, it could be anything. It's mainly the tone of the poem that suggests this romance is irreparable.

It's a long path
My home to yours
I love you so
You are so true
Don't kiss me please
I'm not speaking
I care for you
I don't think so
She's my sister
You don't dress well
Is the spark dead
I've met another

That Mother's Day Moment

You'd call this a poem about a happy time. It's too bad, we at times, have to measure happy times by the moment. The moms were all well pleased, and they left the dance recital fonder than ever, of their daughters. The daughters were well satisfied as well. It was a happy moment for all concerned, mother and daughter.

All was wondrous that one
special moment, the air like a nectar
of sweet ambrosia.
The occasion a dance recital,
on Mother's own day,
and the young dancers were filled with love.
They pirouetted to the rhythmic music,
prancing, and treading, flitting back and forth,
the stage transformed, all heady from the undulating wine.
So much emotion, and fervid bonding.
The mothers understood the pridefulness
and caring oozing from every pore that
Made these girls children
to be cared for.
All was well that Mother's Day moment in time.

The Bras d'Or River

The Bras d'Or River and the Bras d'Or Lakes are both environmental masterpieces. No one and nothing were ever allowed to pollute them. The river itself flows into the North Atlantic and that area is well known for its delectable snow crab and lobster. There are many other plentiful fish stocks as well throughout that region.

The River, in its own right, amazing
First a drop, a splash, then a trickle
Trillions of grass shoots later and still water,
When will it end, ever?
Can we mortals discern
such lofty matters?
Homo sapien and rational,
beings as it were.
Rhetoric and reasoning, reliable discussion
why? how? what? where? who doth of we know?
Water it came somehow, our life giver.
We crave it, we need it.
It is urgent, vital,
And a gift we cannot do without.

Curtain Call

This poem uses the end of a play to substitute for the death of a person. Even some inanimate objects are given human attributes. The poem, by using the play, describes how that person died and is now buried and soon to be forgotten.

When the lights are turned down
And the show is over
The thrill is gone
And the crowd has gone home

When the critical acclaim has ended
For the last performance ever
The red carpet is rolled up
Nothing – a silence of its own

The theater is empty
A sweater a hat a pocket comb left
Mark the past in a
Soon forgotten time while
A floral bouquet loses its petals
Silently dry and wilted
The final bow a quiet exit
A smattering of applause
From somewhere not far away
The show cancelled – the
  Run is over
   All is in darkness
     Quietude forever

Flow On Mira River
Of My Childhood Days

Then it came, the gentle river rolling
Majestic in form, all its beauty glowing.
I saw in the estuary a dreamy sight to behold.
Green water, fish jumping,
Something whispered, enthralling isn't it.
Too good for one such as I,
Yet Paradise unfolded, of what to surmise.
There was a creation I guess, no surprise.
Toronto behind me, just as well.

A delight given to us by what – I can't tell.

As a boy I was a strangling,

Was it my mind or soul something was rearranging.

Many A Beggar's Dream

This poem has a touch of irony in it. The car usurps the person of a man who worked hard to make a lot of money and to lead a great life full of all the best. Then he finds he is getting old and his sins of excess are catching up to him. There the good life ends.

Soundless, smooth, without effort
the car, shiny and black
drove gracefully it's
engine throbbing with power.
what wealth can't buy.

People stared at the furious
elegance and the tires bit
into the asphalt hissing superiority
and passing the lesser machines, riding,
cruising the white lines
with aplomb and assurance and
swallowing up everything in its path.

The pulsating, gleaming
black beast was indomitable until
a piston blew. Much consternation,
such a mess, followed by signs of body rust,
somehow leaking fuel and the engine
seized up. It was over.
the once lusty beast admired and coveted no more.

Such As It Is

A poem which was born out of my childhood poverty. Too many baby Tobins and not enough money. But we had our happier moments. The kids in the poem will be okay, just like we eight, now grown up Tobins are.

Three pairs of tiny eyes
Walk slowly by
Crying inward,
Holding a quarter and
A dime and a nickel
In their little hands,
For the store
To buy lemon drops.
A wee treat
The candy
That will be sweet.

Such is life, joy, then pain,
Sharred remnants
Of another day.
The little ones,
Like a Rembrandt painting,
Porcelain faces
Smile walking home.
Life's not so bad
It's what you make of it,
Tiny eyes, tiny smiles, happy
Till the candy is gone.
Subsistence once again.

The Last Drum

Not trusting Hollywood westerns, I did a little research and decided a narrative poem, a story, allowing for cause and effect, as told by a narrator, may bring a more personal, emotionally involved account of the Indian Wars to my readers. The Indians, at the time, were very proud and felt that living on reserves was an insult.

The air reeked of death, Lone Wolf's soul
withered with each new breath.
Today the grand denouement, the final strife.
There would be many fatalities, and
bloodied corpses, covered in gore.
His family, women and the young,
fled under the cover of night.
They were gone, his people vilified.
Their sin was they were tribal Indians,
no more allowed to roam their own land free.
The U.S. Army honed well in what they did,
sabers hacking, slashing, stabbing,
And the rifles, the ensuing carnage would add to.
The new settlers didn't trust Indians
as the railroad pushed back the frontier.
The Indian Territory, was valuable territory,
and greed motivated Washington throughout.
Sunset, that night, would set on the tribe,
and they would be no more.
The morning fire sputtered its last few embers.
Accept his fate, never!
He would fight till death do part.

He drew close to his blanket his wife had made.
The braves had agreed they would fight the soldiers
and it was that day.
The forest creatures blessed them,
and stayed away, mute in their silence.

Many coups will be counted, a token payment,
for what was taken away.
Tall Elk said to Lone Wolf,
"In our land there are riches we are not
to own. It speaks of we as lesser.
This I tell you so, my friend, my brother."
    Lone Wolf replied, "I grazed my ponies
here and fished in our own river. Now we
go far away to a reservation. It is wrong.
It is an evil thing."
    Tall Elk stood up and said,
"Make them pay with white man's blood."

Sheridan from the north and northeast,
the death march had begun.
General Terry's four thousand, at
the rising of the sun.
Bad whiskey, bad dreams, broken promises,
and now the slaughter.
Each tribe proudly fought their own battles.
Arrows, and war paint, rifles,
but with little ammunition, were all
they had to fight this evil.
The order to be rounded up and taken
away had come but days ago.

Lone Wolf fierce and defiant, raised
his spear on high.
On this day many men would die.
Rifles cracked, shattering the quiet of morn.
The ponies were patted,
it may be their last ride together.
Four hundred and fifty braves,
outnumbered more than ten times over.
War is a hell that always ends.

The camp was set afire, only the braves remained,
all the rest had fled.
The men fought till only forty
were still standing.
The Battleground was a blood red.
The sun set in a red glowing sky.
Lone Wolf, the warrior, as well, perished.

The survivors were marched
south to the dreaded reserve.
The dead, the marchers remembered, as they
walked that lonely walk.
The Indian people considered to be the lesser,
and in their own native land, all so true.

Gunilla Of The Snow White Breast

This poem was inspired by a woman who wrote a love story about her and the assassinated president, John F. Kennedy. She had dated him during the president's first term as a senator. I also mentioned the disparity between the rich and the poor found throughout the world and the problems it causes.

Peeling a mandarin orange
I swallowed
the boudoir
a toy wagon
in Bangladesh
 paint faded
 a wheel missing
 the handle hauling
a kidney coloured chutney
 meat pie
 the hour is late
 in North Hollywood
 the master of the house
 is not returning
 my queen
I swallowed hard
 It was succulent
a tear fell
a baby cried
only death again
only him
he will leave soon
and I shall go with him.

At Least I Had To Marry Her

I contemplate my faithless wife,
The rain pouring, dripping
Off the brim of my bebop cap,
Trickling down my back,
As the cold damp air,
Chills silly me.
Yes, I once tried to fashion
A lasting marriage, out of nothing.

A stranger to the shaving razor.
The wind sifting through
My cheap, threadbare jacket.
Alimony for her while I starve.

The kid I raise through
My child support payments.
Pointless, it is, why do I try.
Tying knots in my shoelaces,
Is less irksome, and more productive.

Just Another Foul Up

Jack Daniels a friend indeed.
I made his acquaintanceship in Vietnam
beguiling, high spirited, an antidote,
for that battlefield haze.
Funny trying to kill people,
but from time immemorial,
there's been battlefields, and battle scars.
Jack Daniels, you are a friend for my need.
Then a damned M.P. took my buddy away;
not likin' it, Jack bashed in his head.
They soon led me away,
no more shootin' for me.
Instead I did some sobering time,
but Jack Daniels, and his prepossessing charms,
will always be a friend of mine.

This Poem Has Been Recycled

One could say, like the poem, we, the human race, are being recycled. Many people believe in reincarnation. The main thing, for now, anyway, is that there is a new generation in place to take over when the time is right.

A dear child is born,
and all is well.
Through blood and pain
arrives a wrinkly little thing,
full of squawks and squirts
and worse.
Sleep, sleep, Oh to sleep
one night through.
Mom and dad have issued
forth, a brand new
member of the human race,
and a grand nephew for I.
Me, my bones grow brittle
and will soon be entombed.
Yet I vindicate my life on earth,
and I do what is right,
to justify my stay amongst
the world wide, polyglot,
human family.
I hope for an easy death,
with one joyful infant
to take my place.
All is well.
Life goes on ever forward.

Ruby of the Green Sky Night

This poem used a despairing mood to make it work. The woman, Ruby, was at the end of her tether and seemed to be lonely and blue, without any sign of help or solace, or sympathy to come to her. At night, the forest can hide some deadly things. It is the western world's answer to the jungle and the inherent dangers within.

The river by the forest
of dead people and frightful sights
sighs out your name.
Come Ruby, forget such desolation,
there is no lover you see,
to call on you.
Eternity calls to your free given death.
The forest hides things
that eat at night,
leaving not one morsel behind,
watching with dead eyes.
The river is your friend,
you with no child – barren.
I know why, I see it, I comprehend.
Plunge Ruby, it is a green sky night.
A life time gained
free of lonely pain.
Walk, choose the river,
go far away
and be nothing again.

Valcartier Prison

This poem reminds me of dramatic flash fiction but in the form of poetry. I was sentenced to Valcartier Military Prison for forty-five days while in the Royal Canadian Air Force. While there, I lost about 35 to 40 pounds and my treatment was brutal. It is still, many years later, the lowest point of my life.

Military prison like a rock
Granite walls, steel bars
monkeys in our cages
was this a military action
or of society or perhaps military society
what did I do, almost nothing.
Yet there I stood, or sat, or walked,
ran, or crawled, for thirty to
ninety days, open custody. It smacked of
an ill mannered military society is what it was.
The soup of the day, a broth
with a few meager vegetables,
enough to fill a soup spoon once, sum total.
What of food, this is Canada.
For supper a saucer full of beans.
I never dreamt I'd be cut off food that
which I always rightfully expected.
Are we degenerating
losing the thin veneer of a civilized world?
What did I do, almost nothing.
I became drunk with an airman
who slapped an airwoman girlfriend's face.
I was nowhere near the incident.
Where was our democracy, why suddenly did I have no rights
Why three months maximum.
The place was hellish, marched double time.
Cleaned the same urinal for hours non-stop.
A miscarriage of justice, common yes,
and I was involved! Where was our human decency
that such preposterousness should happen to me, an honest man.
A military officer heard my case,
he of very little legal training.

Guilty was the verdict but
of what and by who.
I did nothing wrong but to socialize
with a socially incompetent man.

Mrs. Tobin's Magnificent Tree

It is an old house
yet in great repair
left that way by family who care
but the yard between the old house
and a flowing brook
a street, a telephone pole
and near a quiet little nook
it seems can use some work.
The lawn is gone,
Almost, one could say
and that a time ago
until this one busy day
a daughter said to the
old dear – "Mom Tobin
your yard is quite drear."
The daughter planted a
maple tree, and thirty
years later, it towers
over the chewed up yard
tall, statuesque, symmetrical
an enchanting sixty
feet tall.
Foliage in abundance as we all can see
and reeking of health, the lawn is now long
forgotten under Mrs. Tobin's
magnificent maple tree.

Didactic Meanderings

The setting for this poem could be anywhere in a high school facility. I rule out the principal's office, and the graduation ceremony itself, because of the informal nature of this partaking of good advice. The principal, like so many of them, is concerned about his students and is obviously wishing them all the best.

Oh you giddy lighthearted friends,
let you, your beliefs quietly suspend.
perhaps not quite, but what I say is so true.
but particles of it shall seem familiar to you.
It's your graduation year,
partake of the adult world, be brave, and do not fear.
About your brain it's working so don't abuse it
Imbibing in crap you may fall into a pit.
Sure I'm only a high school principal,
I don't know it all and I'm not invincible.
Still I'm no fool,
and you all did just graduate from high school.
Induce into your brain good and pleasant things,
because healthy acts and pleasant practices, your bell rings.
It can and will make a difference,
every little bit helps that's my inference.
As you say hello to adult society,
do it quietly, with a flair for piety.

Sweet and Innocent Is Its Own Reward

Love drops at midnight,
like diamonds shining in your eyes,
I held you like a banker
would hold a bar of gold.
You were the beauty.
Wildly my heart did beat.
The moon glistened
a silvery color,
and we were in love.
We walked past a babbling stream,
And traipsed in unison,
until suddenly appeared,
an antiquated bench
between the hemlock trees.
We soon reclined
and became united as one.
Soon tears trickled down my lover's cheeks;
nineteen and no longer virginal.
I thanked the dewdrops at midnight
for love even half as sweet.

Flow on Beautiful Mira River
While I Praise Your Name

It swept by, thrilling to me,
I the son of a son.
I counted my bones, I the lucky one.
The angel, mother nature's own,
Spake, and said welcome you are.
Do not ever waste away,
And live the way you did.
I have illumined your mind.
See this beautiful river,
Let it always call to you.
Cape Breton the Isle of Gold
You do deserve.
Never a bag of rags,
Or a mind so sore again.
Come, eat lobster, and scallops,
And escape your pain,
Here where you belong.

I Don't Want a Lot in Life
In Any Life

A poem emanating a tone of dissatisfaction. It's about hard work for little recompense in the way of a decent and happy life. The overall mood of the poem is one where day-to-day living is almost futile because of no happiness.

A Stygian gravesite,
underground an unstable mine shaft.
Digging out coal,
eating dirt, breathing in coal dust,
lungs, infested, black.
To make a living,
what won't men do.

A trucker up at four a.m.
humping freight by five.
Muscle and ligaments, sinews straining,
bones, grinding, popping.
On the road churning up the miles,
behind the wheel, behind in his bills,
fighting back at extinction.
He returns to an empty life.
The kids stare at the T.V.,
the soaps tell them a better story.
Mom on the phone,
no time for the husband of the hour,
why does he bother?
He takes a drink, and begins to wonder,
this way he can live another day,
and do the same thing tomorrow.
Why – well, we're trapped – and no way out!
Live on, until you fall off
of your topsy turvy wheel,
and then you are no more.

The Island of Sweet Breezes

The roiling blue seas
Spewing their eternal breezes
My soul aches to escape,
To do the other thing.
I once presumed,
Yet now I reminisce,
The young have soft hearts
Youth not wasted on they.
Puppy dogs are happy,
Stars come out in the dark;
If we knew, if only we did.
The wind is soft
And breast milk warm.

The Masterful Uncaring Machines

He's reputed to be middle eastern.
Yeah, sure, so we're told.
The master manipulator could be anywhere.
He'll take your filthy lucre,
every penny, and he'll turn it into gold.
This is all beneath his dignity of course,
so righteous and God like is he, ah hummm.
He's makin' it all the world over.
Insert the nozzle,
push that button,
get your fix,
the machine with no qualms does what it's told.
Just one more source, tout le monde.
What else is new.
Give it some thought.
There may be an answer somewhere out there.

Here We Go Again

First came the egg,
then the gluten.
Next came the gun
and it was shootin'.
Next the doctor, and his painful slap;
followed by a warm breast,
and a cozy, snuggly nap.
Daddy was next, and he
held her in his lap.
Love began to flow like beer,
it was always on tap.

The Rural Route

I would describe this poem as bucolic in nature, and would classify it as a pastoral poem. Its setting is rural America, near the turn of the 19th century, into the 20th. It would just as easily fit in Canada as well. Until the dirty thirties, close to twenty-five percent of the population of Canada depended on the family farm for support.

Diddy and his son, Rory,
they work from morn,
till the moon, the sky does adorn.
Cows abed, milking done.
crack open a beer, it hisses like squirts of milk.
let sleep come for a comforting visit.
such a life, a hard way to
eke out a living.
the barnyard rat, ah,
watch him, some leeway be giving.
the young in school learning,
the new school marm, knowledge returning.
wife at home where she likes to be,
wearing her brand new apron.
cows in the barn, mooing, and settling in,
the woodstove throwing a warm, flaming red heat.
rural is the life to live.
love your family,
gather your friends by the hearth.
have forgiveness for your enemies
or so the Good Book doth impart.

Vintage Sherry Wine

A sip from a glass
Chipped and dusty
Love was blooming
And the corkscrew at the ready.
A cacophony of sound
Poured from further up the street
Oh for a melody, ever so sweet.
But would the glass
Be drained; it was
A very good year.
A sip, just a nip
Something with a bite;
It would sop up the dust
From a little war baby tyke.
Wine is heady, and love itself,
Out in the open
And off the shelf.

A. B. See
A New Twist on Remembering

The ABCs

(A) - Was an Arab, who made quite a din.
(B) - Was a Beggar man, ragged and thin.
(C) - Was a Candy man, who sold lots of sweets.
(D) - Was a Drunkard, who slept in the streets.
(E) - Was an Elf, who danced like a fairy.
(F) - Was a Fox, so cunning and wary.
(G) - Was a German, who drank lots of beer.
(H) - Was a Hunter, who killed a deer.
(I) - Was an Indian, who shot with a bow.
(J) - Was a Juggler, who put on a great show.
(K) - Was a Knight, with a very sharp lance.
(L) - Was a Lady, who learned how to dance.
(M) - Was a Music man, who played many tunes.
(N) - Was a Nobleman, who lived by the dunes.
(O) - Was an Ostrich, with very long legs.
(P) - Was a Pigeon, who laid little blue eggs.
(Q) - Was a Quaker, who wore a red vest.
(R) - Was a Robin, who built a strong nest.
(S) - Was a Soldier, who fought in the war.
(T) - Were the Tides that washed on the shore.
(U) - Was an Usher, who showed you your seat.
(V) - Was a Valet, so tidy and neat.
(W) - Was a Whisper, whispered without any tones.
(X) - Was an X-Ray, that pictured your bones.
(Y) - Was a Youth, who played the bagpipes.
(Z) - Was a Zebra with black and white stripes.

The Eternal Tryst

Sure it wasn't the beach at Malibu. As a matter of fact it wasn't even in California. Actually, she was a brunette but that's what artistic imagination, or say, poetic license is all about. Wouldn't you say!

Tendrils of golden warmth fell
on her luscious visage
her pink top enshrined
her full beautiful breasts
her delicious lips were
attired in shocking pink lipstick
and sweat lined the fine flaxen hairs
just above her upper lip
I could feel me becoming moist
The sky was a baby blue
with the clouds fully animated
and flitting by like cars on
the Santa Monica freeway
we walked the beach in Malibu
the hot sand seemed to whisper
there is hardly anyone here
except we two
her silky white shorts revealed
well developed legs with perfect thighs
we sat on the beach the sky above
and earth, our home, below
like Adam and Eve so many generations ago.
The Pacific Ocean declined away from we
the two eternal lovers
from time immemorial
here to register our lusty infatuation
for each other as
per customary from one generation
of mankind to the blessed successors
until death the final aparting.

The Egg and I

The egg
        cultivated –
              The sperm assisted
           Pax Vobiscum,
                 Child of the
                          beastly
          A joy toy
                    Commodity

Life
   from
      borning
  preparations
     A trajectory
                 bursts
     Baby had arrived
           The deed performed
Guilt pain

Tiny particle
          A living sliver
                         Soulful and sinful
The fateful mingle
     No future plan
    Fear life death

The Empty Port

This poem picks at our sense, for example, 'Oh to plunge' or 'snake oil medicine man'. The sailor whose home port really is empty is obviously trying to thrash it out at sea. But life has given him such a raw deal he wonders about how much more of this he can take. Unfaithful lovers are the most hurtful kind.

I'm just a lovelorn young sailor,
My once true love shanghaied me.
I'm aboard my ship, a captive of the lonely sea.
Oh to plunge, and no longer be.
If there should be a God up in heaven,
Then I plead that you shorten my span.
She proved to be a faithless lover.
She left me for a snake oil medicine man.

A Diamond In The Rough

This poem is all about how easy it is for a fledgling romance to go sour. I guess as a musician, he had his head in the clouds for too long. The phrase 'amour propre' is an old expression meaning your ego went off somewhere temporarily, I hope. But such is life.

What can it mean,
A waitress so luscious
Like a diamond, sensual and shiny,
Masterfully crafted, and
Finessed to perfection.
Me a musician on the tourist trail.
Wanting a bite and a glass of ale,
Never say ever, never again.
All tanned and simpering, the crowd sat.
And my buddy, my electric base,
Heard my heart thumping,
Da dum da dum.
The world's oldest rhythm,
Can she be done – me,
With such a voluptuous creation.
Smiling, over she came.
I sat there tongue tied,
My amour propre, damn it,
had abandoned me.
Even my argot fled,
And no hope of a passable cant.
No mawkish laughter,
Instead she did her thing.
She took my order,
And I never saw her again.

The Princess

This poem was inspired in part by an Australian poem written during the 1930s. What I did to give certain human attributes to an animal. This branch of poetry quite often leads to surprise endings. This poem did have a pleasantly happy ending but I like movies with similar endings as well.

Anne was her name.
Like a queen she was, but
a princess really, and now in trouble.
A man had kidnapped her.
He had been seen leaving
her castle and dragging Anne with him.
Where was she now, perhaps in
some tower dungeon, or an
isolated compound, or a
well-guarded retreat hideout.
Her family was horrified;
they'd do anything for her safe return.
A young boy Duke Jonathan heard of this,
and the generous reward for freeing
the princess, and her safe return home.

The young duke, as he was known, attacked the search
with all his vigor, taking chances,
and never easing up – such dedication
Under tragic circumstances.
Young Anne was found
for sale in a pet shop, such degradation.
But better that than an animal shelter.
the princess soon was returned home.
She jumped into her litter box,
happy to be back,
and dined on tuna supreme.
She then curled up on
her satin pillow and slept restfully
until the next morning.

The Dancing Daughter

So young, so sweet,
So cute and petite.
Sequined dress, back scooped out,
Slippers flawlessly caressing the floor in rote.
Dance, dance, please do okay,
The recital is today.
Such applause, a thrill to recall.
So beautiful, like Sleeping Beauty at the ball.
Well made up to perfection, in honor of,
That precious woman, the object of your love.
Cameras clicking,
Anticipation quickening.
I thank you daughter for honoring me.
I, and we all, your devotion did see,
On this most memorable Mother's Day.

The Churning Waters

The location for this poem is Louisburg, Nova Scotia. It is one of Canada's most visited historic sites. This is where the early French settlers first met the English usurpers who won Canada for the British Crown. In many parts of Canada, the French and English live side by side but quite often there is a sense of separation between the two. This poem also speaks of the aloneness in today's world.

Two small islets in Louisbourg Harbour,
estranged, yet side by side.
The cold, briny, water splashes over
the two, jutting, rough edged, clumps of rock,
Separate like a broken love, fallen away.

A woman, husbandless, past the lighthouse road,
visited by a blast of wind screaming its fury.
Her lover gone, a seabound rover,
the wind blows mercilessly, come home, come back.
Omnipotent, dictatorial, the chasm, non negotiable.

The two petite islands, firmament, rock hard – in French
'La Belle Dame Sans, Clémence.' A bastion by the fortresses shore,
and 'Queen Anne's Isle' ruling the changing tides.
The islets, separate, and distinct, and unchanging.
The water swirls, foaming, and angry.
Do not take liberties, history has been made here.

A sweet dream, and an old photo, like a laser beam,
pierces the loveless void, for a heart stopping moment.
No consoling welcome home still,
not a comforting word, or a loving gesture.
Alone yet never all alone,
isolated, till the furious storm,
blows out to sea.

The Reading Lamp

I had, for a few years, tried to intellectualize my beliefs and emotions with limited success. This poem 'The Reading Lamp' is my first poem written after I decided to aim for other markets besides the literary quarterlies. This poem, and others written more recently, are the result of a more simplistic writing style. This poem is more me.

The light from the reading lamp
illuminated the darkened room.
The light, but what light, and
from where did it come.
Inspired perhaps by sunlight,
a dream of mankind; a
simplified candle power,
with a gleaming bright light
which could beam all night,
without a flicker, or burning out.
I could read my book in the
middle of the night, waiting for
peacefulness, and a soundless quietude.
The lamp is turned off, and I
lie there in the darkened room,
waiting for sleep to come.

Watch Your Sinful Ways

Tiger brute, your eyes aglare.
From your gruesome fury, let I be spared.
Unfettered you await the direful kill.
Fear you evoke from all,
You, most intimidating beast of the jungle way.
Horrendous, your growl, as you pounce.
Nightmarish are the disfigured remains;
To you but another eerie meal.
Other creatures mark you as the formidable one.
Alarmed, and frightened, they remain.
You rule the jungle fearfully so.

A Sailor's Last Love

This poem I remember well. It was inspired by the American folk singer Jimmy Rogers. When I heard the song for the first time a few years ago, I immediately decided to write a poem based approximately on the song.

When my sailing days were over
I dreamt of coming home to you
A rainbow in the sky did hover
And I wished my love stayed true
The stars in the sky like diamonds
And the moon a glistening hue
Then I saw your image dancing
Like my heart in love with you.

Johnny's Mother

I have fond memories of this poem. It was the second one I wrote and the first I had published. It was written about my mother just as old age was seriously settling in. If you're into pathos or like sentiment, then give it a read.

The starlings who
nest in your love
filled home, are
all that know you
are now all alone.

Your husband, gently,
has passed on
and your children
well grown, have gone.

No one sees now
your china blue eyes,
as blue as the
teacups, on your
wedding day arrived.

Now only the starlings
know you are
there alone, and they
sing you to sleep,
Till the last bird is flown.

In The Velvet Night

This is another pastoral poem full of vivid description and elements that quicken our senses. Here on Cape Breton Island, the living is easy and good in the summertime. The Island isn't that far south of the Arctic so winters can be difficult. One can easily enjoy himself (herself) any time. It is a way of life all of its own.

In the silky darkness of the Inverness sky
I sat reposed on an old tree stump
In front of my girlfriend Karen's homestead
The stars had started to puncture the black velvet night
Soon came a cluster of the beguiling little fires above the earth
Silver was their gleam and the moon shone on
Looking so majestic yet a mystery unknown
What were they really would we humans ever know
I sat, hardly a sound to be heard
Then a cry mingled freely with the stillness
It was a hootie owl truly in his element
The goodnight howl of a wild cat bedding down
The wind blew faintly, softly
Whispering through the trees
Squirrels safely in their bowers in the darkness sublime
The sky swept up to the top of the world
And then down to my sweaty toes
Just barely I could see my forest neighbor next door
Cow tracks aplenty and wood chips scattered about
Tomorrow was another day
Would the light of day again come
And would joy come or with it sorrow bring

A Vignette – Peanuts

I finished writing this vignette and took it to my typist. I knew there was a girl in the comic strip, it's just that I couldn't remember her name. On walking home from my typist's, I remembered, Lucy. Too late.

Snoopy Sez   –   Charlie Brown
                                        Pull up your socks
                                        And watch out for rocks
                                        Rake the leaves
                                        Before the neighborhood grieves
                                        We're a fire hazard

Charlie Brown Sez –   The leaves
                                        Won't catch fire
                                        And I'm not for hire
                                        Besides it's gonna rain

Snoopy Sez   –   You're still little Charlie. Do it
                                        Get busy and not a peep
                                        While on this porch I sleep

Charlie Brown Sez –   It's not raining yet
                                        But soon I bet

Charlie hooks the garden hose up
Snoopy was dumb even as a pup
Charlie tugs on his blanket and
Up to the roof he goes
Turns on the nozzle
At the tip of the hose
Sprays the still sleeping Snoopy
Who wakes and sez this is poopy
Then he sez 'it is raining after all'
He goes back to sleep and Charlie has a ball
Off he goes to catch up on his T.V.

The Debutante

A slinky, silvery, gown
Like she had always dreamt of.
Her dark hair, pinioned
By a diamond tiara.
An ivory cameo brooch,
On a black velvet band,
Around her long, graceful, neck.
Her bejeweled bracelet, once glittery,
Dulled by the light from the stars.
A wino propped up in front
Of the four star restaurant,
Gave mute testimony to
This deluxe babe, but
Her mind deluded by drugs.
The police – but they were
Reading her rights to her.
It wasn't such a long trip after all,
From street kid to the deed to
A rooming house in her name.
Drugs had done her in.
A shoplifting charge too.
Tonight's trip had gone sour
The cops had closed her act down again.

The First Snow

The white flakes fell
From the heavens, as the
Angels fluttered their wings.
Tiny cherubic school children
Trudged cheerily through
The drifting snow
Their hearts aglow,
Laughing and smiling,
With each step.
Innocent of bitterness and rancor,
The home fire soon to embrace
The chilled young tykes.
Joyful and caring and the hearth
Will make their tiny spirits soar.
Branches crackled overhead,
The frosty chill had set in
Icicles, and bitter wind,
The snow piled up deep.
With a steady gait they pressed on,
Till safe shelter was gained.

Something Witty

I write a column,
of sorts, while my best friends
sneer. It's not a parody,
well it's sort of queer,
as oddities come on
this planet mirth.
Politics I deride, the
economy quizzical.
I try to remain a
jovial animale.
I mock nothing, yet
a travesty I'm described.
Such discourtesy, but
they still laugh up their sleeve.
I rail, and banter, yet
browbeat no one.
As for marriage,
the one thing my
funny bone can't handle.
A figure of fun,
a column of burlesque,
but I tell you this
chaff must end.
If we don't straighten up,
then the planet mirth
will become the planet dearth,
and mock that if you can.

The Water Nymph

Lorelia, spirit of the waterways,
Temptress to all seagoing men.
The land mass in peril.
May I safely ply your waters,
With salt in my veins,
And roaming, with eyes alert,
Searching, and fearing,
Looking, for flesh and blood
To cling to, rather than
Ice water, and frigid hearts.

Bad Boys

This poem is similar to a mid-50s rock 'n roll tune by a group who struck a chord, as it were, with the song, amongst the young. Whenever a D.J. would play the tune, four or five young boys or more, would call the station asking the D.J. to play it again. Sales were good as well. I don't know why, but perhaps you can tell.

Oh yeah oh yeah oh yeah
There's the girls, oh yeah oh yeah
Everyone knows there's no such thing as
Ba ad boys ba ad boys ba ad boys
The little bastards will steal you blind
They'll rip off your property
Oh yeah oh yeah oh yeah
Ba aa ad boys ba aa ad boys
Females are what – sorta but
They like their boys ba ad
Oh yeah oh yeah oh yeah
Watch out he could be killa magilla
Ba ad boys ba ad boys ba ad boys
If he needs loot he'll rob a bank
The warden like a father
Ba aa ad ba aa ad   ba aa ad boys
Just be bad that's all he can do

Shaken Leaf Syndrome

This could best be described as a pastoral poem involving Mother Nature at work. In my own home town, almost all of the shade trees became infected with Dutch elm disease. The story, as it is told, about the suspended tree leaf, is true. Briefly I suspected a miracle. Then along came a spider and with the tree diseased and all, the leaf was lucky to have survived, as long as it did.

The discarded brown leaf
Severed from its family tree
Part of a Dutch elm tree
Rife with disease
Dead of its own worth, prematurely
And its former mates, the
Branches, ruined and dying too

If the wind blows just right
And it huffs and hurls
You the bud of a branch
To old Mrs. Dudley's lawn may blow
Mayhap a tiny gene or two
Will surface in the chain of life
A blade of grass
Gone but never forgotten
For eons and then
All is anew

You fought your end deservingly
Yet dying so it seemed
But the fickle winds swooped
You aloft once more, dancing, you
Twirled animated and still there

Then a power line
Embraced you ever briefly as you fell
Like man and mother nature did in times before
But snared you were
By a spider's web
And lunch you were to be
But the winds of good fortune
Roared and howled and
Blew the shriveled leaf away.

It Never Works Right

Here intimate descriptiveness was employed to set the stage for love's sweet sorrow. The petals plucked from the flower were used to substitute for the poet slowly undressing his dream girl who he dearly loved. Slightly older, and some younger women as well, liked this poem.

In a little white chapel
by the side of a road
lined with weeds and
chirping linnets overhead
frightened I slipped inside
and picked one flower
the one I had lost
and fell in love did I
all over again.
Ah but the sweet ambrosia
of loves heady wine
I breathed deep the wafting
perfumed air
beauty everywhere
and she so fair.
abuse pretold had clouded my mind
blood that day was
shed the second time.
a pink carnation crimson red splattered
kissed by golden rays
falling from between darkened clouds.
I plucked the petals one after another
until I was pierced and bleeding
a thorn had penetrated my being
from the quivering
naked slender stem.
It was the other man after all
waiting at the high holy alter
yet I did not love in vain.

I had loved her but lost my all.
Now I sit here
and shudder in pain
no physician has a cure
no medicine will do.
No not she but t'was I
who found I was mentally ill ,
because I could never confront her
about the love in my heart
for one so beautiful as she.

Madame Anastasia

This poem was written as a lament to my mother who had just died a few hours previously. I used a metaphor to explain mom's true nature and her lovely personality. She meant a lot to her family and friends. We all miss her.

Not the Milan Opera House
Nor the Lincoln Center now,
But sings she does, for her older admirers
And those, with her, still in love.
She hits the high notes and
We are thrilled, but alas
Her age has slown her down.
Performances, she sings a little less, but more beautiful,
A work of joy and love, and strife and pain.
She is still our only one
We come to see her now,
Any performance could be her last.
But we loved her through it all
Dear Madame Anastasia, you touch our souls
Till your performance ends.

Another Well Salted Wound

Will not the door open,
Shining in the light.
Fold the curtains
Shielding your mind.
Open your heart,
And learn to care,
From a social outsider, misfit, schizophrenic,
To this generation of enlightened thoughts.
Forget your barbed conjecture,
Kinship it's a whole new world.
Our new order
Can learn to care for all.

There Were No Losers

This poem was written about an imaginary poetry contest I once thought might be a nice way to celebrate Canada's 150th *birthday coming up soon.*

I imbibed in the poetry tonight
all so blissful we did it up right
a rapturous evening for we all
true Cape Breton Island best, I danced at the ball
many delicious poems I heard recited,
my heart is light, I'm thrilled and delighted.
Why bow before a church steeple
excitement courses like whisky in people.
T'is but heaven if I may judge.
I say of the losers, don't hold a grudge
'Nuff' said at the steelworkers hall,
I the MC veritably full of gall.
Even of the average poetics, I'm so proud;
you the audience electrifyingly loud.
One must allow for the bin reduced to clear
To me I shall hold the affair so dear

Ode to the Atlantic

A poem about something that runs the gamut from the sacred to the sublime. The human race, as we know it, couldn't exist without the Atlantic. It cleanses our continent, our rivers and harbors; brings the wind; in part, shelters much marine life; and provides us with considerable transportation. It is a mighty thing.

Wind blown
And ice shorn
Atlantic water; ferment
Of unconquerable might,
Powerful, secretive, primordial
Eternal benefactor – life giver.
Cold, unfeeling, from now,
Till times of yore.
Wonderment of the planet,
Deep, dead, a poem in itself
In eternal motion.
Death and star crossed lovers.
The ocean, a sailor's pain.
Flow on, oh mighty brine
We bow to your greatness,
O' wonder primeval,
Our gift you maintain.

'Vincent I With You Go'

Part I

Speaking wishing crying begging for what?
Jerking pulling teasing dreaming habitual?
Hoping praying loving who? What for?
Lusting (why?) seeing (alas!) breaking (yes)
Throwing selling asking – panderer?
Snapping filthy foulness
Shaming mending frustrating (artistic)

Part II

To you and our mutual creator
in my own defence
I gave myself back to you unreservedly
a premeditated decision
don't do this to me again
I thought it out clearly
I could only paint
for what that's worth
I painted what I saw
what I saw there it is see
leave me along – surely
let me die
you are imposing on me
such insolence
I won't be ashamed
of you anymore.

Te Deum Da Da

This poem is just an extension of the experimental art and films from the sixties and seventies. Andy Warhol and his painting of a soup can was one of the better known examples of this kind of art. My poem is a general non-specific story of a romance gone sour. The poet blames the other person — but true love comes from knowing and understanding.

Tiny bluebird how why
deliriums but surely your mate
world's apart no you (all)
I'm freezing ice in my throat damn it I skate

No nest in a cave underneath remotely
yours is full of all good things
my lover corporal bodass to demote me
she wasn't aware of pyramids and moonlit sultry things

Like a magic inverted apocalypse not **surly**!
is my tiny bluebird **warrior** of believers
I loved my mate surely a meeting
of the mind's deathlike cough **then** an answer

Ah blue Spartan dancer in the sky
there will be other chances
yon dilettante tasted fox meat stones he's high
Sympatico I'm wired up to other romances

The Last Voyage

I was a lonely sailor,
Out on the deep, vast, sea,
When I heard my true
Love calling to me.

I saw the stars shining
In her beautiful hair.
They glimmered like her eyes,
Her heart full of love for me.

I dreamt of her so vividly,
My soul filled with pain.
She had died in childbirth,
That mal night, of a downpouring rain.

Must I jump to my death,
Was she asking me to die.
Call out to me, my lover my wife,
Illuminate my mind, tell me what to do.

Will it be you and I,
Or me, and the ocean so blue.

'A Gift – Not a Miracle'

In a land far away,
the America of my youth, say,
or exotic Babylon, lush and fragrant, rivers flowing through paradise.
I saw myself come frigid as ice.
Youthful strife, a wielded knife, by a cold grimy hand
am I to escape this forbidding dessert land?
Purgatory, prisons, mental hospitals all crazy anyway,
perhaps cometh to me a new and startling day.
Oh to hold a woman as I did at the time of my youth,
take her home, caress her, and kiss her hard on her mouth!
The angel of death mayhap died
or to me perchance it lied.
There is an emergence, like a resurrection come over me.
Happy tomorrows, full of beauty, and I shall observe and see.

Nightlife Down at the Seniors' Apartments

This was written August of 2012 while sitting on a chair in front of the seniors' residence where I live. It was a comfortable night to be out. All the tenants were in good cheer. The poem, because of the abundance of inspiration, took only three drafts to finish.

The sky was as clear as a young child's mind.
The breeze enriched a cozy warmth.
It wasn't a sticky heat but we didn't itch much.
Dormant sires and dams were we.
For some it's always nice, but not as sweet as a pleasant memory.
Old age t'is but that last blessing
And to we, comes an understanding and tolerance.
Our lore of knowledge forces down barriers,
Such as resentment and argumentation.
Then forgiveness flows sweetly from the heart, and soul,
Something that pleases me greatly.
As the sun rises and sets, we've seen another day.
It is all we can ask at any age.
There is that human bond for all ages.
We make our peace with God and
Old scars have a way of being mended.
It always ends well; there is a dignity in death.
And with the spirit of The Master,
In its peace, we do dwell.

Dirty Waters

This poem is basically a metaphor, where a storm is used to substitute for a woman's, deep, hating anger for her boyfriend. Also, a simile is used for her boyfriend just past the last half of the poem, to add to the literal and figurative mix-up. Perhaps I give too much information on the metaphorical substitution for it to be a classic metaphor.

The storm its fury mounting,
The sea tosses about,
With its waves in high contempt
Of sailor lads, braving the danger,
And looking for safe harbor,
In the mad gale.
Tree leaves, and branches,
Shake from the fierce, brutal force,
Of the deadly storm.
It is like a woman,
Gone amok, losing her temper
And the wind does still blow.
Her hair whips over her head,
Caused by the hating force of
Her emotional agitation.
The kinetic energy engulfs her being,
As she loses all control,
And the pitiless storm rages on savagely.

Here We Live As We Can

Nature nurtures waters offspring
Fish and trees and bucolic greenery
Clear, like the air water flows briskly
In its rush to melt the winter's snow
Then purposely it gushes forth to the ocean
And voids like a religious devotion
Ever unwavering for many eons
Then there surely is an overall plan
Humanity must go on rightly so
For a successful and a successive generation
One woman one man procreation

The Sweet Things in Life

This poem uses the iambic pentameter method of balancing each line of poetry. There should be five short syllables and five long syllables in each line. Also, I went with rhyming couplets at the end of each line. It is in praise of the female figure and the male reaction to it.

Plump, adorable, pleasing, sugar plums
slurpy, like strawberries and cream, no crumbs.
thrilling, like an orgasm, O lovely mine,
precious to me, eat your fill off the vine.
so thrilling, like Carnival, let it be,
ambrosial sex, nectar from the tree.
captivating, a full, fleshy, plum you see.
hung by the Elysium garden Deity.

Epilogue

By Richard K. Tobin, Author

Well, now that you've read my book of poetry, I stand here fully exposed. I bared it all including bits and pieces of my soul. Now, perhaps, you know I never was one for keeping secrets. Still, I have led a quiet life. I started that early in life and then as a young adult, I had a bout with depression that hit me between the eyes.

The doctors were of some help; more than one of them were a big help to me. However, I waged my own war with my fair-sized mental difficulties and kept on winning battle after battle.

As things went better for me early on, I found many useful things I could do. One of these was taking a re-interest in reading, and then came the writing bug, sometime later on.

I hope the book was of some use to you. At least, if nothing else, you can always say you read another book of poetry. I made more friends that way. Overall, it's proven to be kind of a charming effort. Say maybe I'm a leprechaun and I'm completely harmless. So is the book.